Spiritual Warfare for a Soul

A Bible Study Guide

by Dr. Candice Vietzke & Michael Vietzke

Disciples of God Publishing
Bend, OR

Copyright © 2013 by Michael & Dr. Candice Vietzke

Spiritual Warfare for a Soul: A Bible Study Guide
Printed in the United States of America

ISBN # 978-0-9893337-3-3

All rights reserved solely by the authors. The authors guarantee all content is original and does not infringe upon the legal rights of any other person or work. No part of this book may be reproduced in any form without the permission of the authors. The views expressed in this book are not necessarily those of the publisher. Unless otherwise indicated, Bible quotations are taken from The King James Version.

Scripture quotations marked (NIV) are taken from the Holy Bible, New International Version®, NIV®. Copyright © 1973, 1978, 1984, 2011 by Biblica, Inc.™ Used by permission of Zondervan. All rights reserved worldwide. www.zondervan.com The "NIV" and "New International Version" are trademarks registered in the United States Patent and Trademark Office by Biblica, Inc.™

Scripture quotations marked ESV are taken from The Holy Bible, English Standard Version® (ESV®)
Copyright © 2001 by Crossway, a publishing ministry of Good News Publishers. All rights reserved. ESV Text Edition: 2011

Scripture quotations marked NASV are taken from the New American Standard Bible. Copyright © 1960, 1962, 1963, 1968, 1971, 1972, 1973, 1975, 1977, 1995 by the Lockman Foundation. Used by permission. (www.Lockman.org).

Scripture quotations marked (NLT) are taken from the Holy Bible, New Living Translation, copyright © 1996, 2004, 2007 by Tyndale House Foundation. Used by permission of Tyndale House Publishers, Inc., Carol Stream, Illinois 60188. All rights reserved.

Scripture quotations marked Amplified Bible are taken from The Holy Bible, The Amplified Bible. Copyright © 1965. Used by permission.
All scripture quotations marked Word English Bible™ are public domain.

Scripture quotations marked (TNIV) are taken from Today's New International Version. Copyright © 2005 by Biblica, Inc.™ Used by permission of Zondervan. All rights reserved worldwide. www.zondervan.com The "NIV" and "New International Version" are trademarks registered in the United States Patent and Trademark Office by Biblica, Inc.™

Scripture quotations marked The Holy Bible, Easy to Read Version. Copyright© 2006 by World Bible Translation Center. Used by permission. All rights reserved.

WARNING

You are entering into a Bible study that teaches you how to confront the enemy. The enemy sees this as an attack and will do everything in his power to stop you. Whether you need help with evil spiritual forces that are currently tormenting you or you are an addict, or surviving an addictive relationship or need to have your eyes opened to see the spiritual warfare that envelopes us every day. Whether you need guidance and wisdom to reach the lost and plant the seeds of knowledge to save them from hell. Or maybe you yourself may need forgiveness for your sins in order to seek a relationship with the living God, for it is only through His forgiveness and grace that we can be saved. God has brought this study to you for a reason. My advice is to carefully pray and seek God before starting this study and ask God for protection from the enemy. Everyone can find that ultimate relationship with the Lord through salvation, for it is only through him that we can we truly conquer evil.

Table of Contents

Chapter 1	The Battle Begins	1
Chapter 2	The Road to Hell	10
Chapter 3	Visions of Demons	22
Chapter 4	Demons Smell Death	34
Chapter 5	Heaven or Hell	43
Chapter 6	Angels and Demons	53
Chapter 7	Demons Fight for Their Prize	61
Chapter 8	The Journey Home	66
Chapter 9	The Acceptance of Christ	72
Chapter 10	The Armor of God	80
Chapter 11	The Final Battle	87
Chapter 12	It Is Finished	94

Chapter 1

The Battle Begins

This chapter speaks of our enemy Satan and his evil schemes. The Bible tells us in Ephesians 6:12 that our fight is not against flesh and blood, but against the rulers, the authorities, the powers of this dark world and against the spiritual forces of evil in the heavenly realms.

1. How does this verse make you look at the problems or conflicts in your life differently?

_____

_____

_____

_____

_____

_____

_____

_____

_____

2. When confronted with an impossible situation do you see through your spiritual eyes as Elisha did or do you tend to look around in defeat as the servant did?

_____

_____

_____

_____

_____

_____

_____

_____

3. God has a perfect plan for each of ours lives. But as imperfect people we tend to mess it up by giving into temptations by the choices we make. What regrets, mistakes or choices did you make that sent you on a different path than the one God had planned for you?

_____

_____

_____

_____

_____

4. When faced with a challenge or an opponent what do you do to prepare to meet or face it?

5. Do you think the American dream has weakened our focus on the command Jesus gave us to go into all the world and make disciples? Why or Why not?

_____

_____

_____

_____

_____

_____

_____

_____

_____

_____

_____

_____

_____

_____

_____

_____

_____

_____

6. If money were no object, what would you do differently in your life to fulfill Matthew 28:16-20?

7. Monetarily, do you think you are rich? By what standard do you use to determine if you are rich or poor?

8. If God asked you to sell all your belongings and go and preach the gospel, truthfully what would you do?

9. Hind site is 20/20, If LuAnn had known that first day she took a drink that it would destroy her and her family, I believe she would have done things differently. How does looking back on your own life now at the small temptations that caused you to sin and produce problems in your life that some will struggle with until we die and most of us would change affect the way you look at those temptations today? Does the pleasures of the moment outweigh the consequences of the future? How can you use this to rethink any temptation that comes your way in the future?

Chapter 2

The Road to Hell

This chapter talks about living for yourself and not for God and how Satan uses our fleshly desires against us.

"Hell and destruction are never full; so the eyes of man are never satisfied."
Proverbs 27:20 (KJV).

1. Have you tried to fill the space in your heart meant for Jesus with something else? Why doesn't it work?

_____
_____
_____
_____
_____
_____
_____
_____
_____
_____
_____
_____

2. Do you believe that demons rejoice when you do something wrong? Why or why not?

3. According to Galatians 5:17 we are constantly at war inside ourselves. How does giving into temptations affect this daily tug-o-war?

_____
_____
_____
_____
_____
_____
_____
_____
_____
_____
_____
_____
_____
_____
_____
_____
_____
_____
_____
_____

4. In Romans 8:3-5 Paul talks about having weak flesh and why we need Jesus as our savior. When we live in the flesh our minds are set on fleshly desires, but when we walk in the Spirit our minds are set on what the Spirit desires. How can we overcome our flesh and walk in the Spirit?

5. Jesus warned us in Ephesians 4:27 not to give the devil a foothold? What can or will happen if you do?

_____
_____
_____
_____
_____
_____
_____
_____
_____
_____
_____
_____

6. 1 Peter warns us to guard against the attacks of Satan. Do you think it is smart to flirt with temptation and give into ungodly practices and ask for forgiveness later? Why or why not?

_____
_____
_____
_____

7. Are you someone who believes that people who are over cautious about demons being in everything or are you aware that demons try to entice you daily away from the things of God and toward an eternity in hell? Why or Why not?

8. We often look to the 10 commandments to find the law that guides us, but Galatians 5:19-21 lists the wrong things the sinful self does and we should avoid. Have you ever looked at the Bible and declared some things to be grey areas? Or ignored or brushed them aside ? Why is that a great deceit Satan uses?

9. Which of these areas in Galatians 5:19-21 do you need to work on? Pray and let the Holy Spirit speak to you in this area.

10. Why do you think God gave us weaknesses?

_____
_____
_____
_____
_____
_____
_____
_____
_____
_____

11. Write about the power God gives us over the demons. How do we get this power? Do you want to possess this power? Why?

_____
_____
_____
_____
_____
_____
_____

12. According to Matthew 17:20 if you have faith what is impossible for you? Do you truly believe that? Why or why not? Why do you think Jesus used a mountain in this passage? (If you struggle in this area pray to God and read this scripture and others to increase your faith.)

_____

_____

_____

_____

_____

_____

_____

_____

_____

_____

_____

_____

_____

_____

_____

_____

_____

Chapter 3

Visions of Demons

This chapter tells us why and how we should test the spirits to see if they are from God or from Satan.

"Dear friends, do not believe every spirit, but test the spirits to see whether they are from God, because many false prophets have gone out into the world. This is how you can recognize the Spirit of God: Every spirit that acknowledges that Jesus Christ has come in the flesh is from God, but every spirit that does not acknowledge Jesus is not from God."

1 John 4:1–3 (NIV)

1. According 1 John 4:1-3 how do we test or recognize the Spirit of God?

2. According to Deuteronomy 18:9-12 what does God find detestable? Why?

3. If these things are detestable in God's eyes should we have anything to do with these things if they are in a book, a movie or on TV even if we are not engaged in the activity itself? Why or why not?

4. Do you believe in Satan? Why do you or do you not believe?

5. Do you believe that idols, dream catchers, and other occult items can have demons attached to them? Why or why not?

6. What do you think about the current reality shows that hunt "ghosts" and other supernatural phenomenon? Do you believe that demons are the cause of some of the occurrences seen or heard on the shows?

_____
_____
_____
_____
_____
_____
_____
_____
_____
_____
_____
_____
_____
_____
_____
_____
_____

7. Have you had an encounter with something unnatural as a child or an adult that you can look back on now and say that you were in the presence of a demon?

_____
_____
_____
_____
_____
_____
_____
_____
_____
_____
_____
_____

8. Did anyone ever teach you how to confront a demon if attacked?

_____
_____
_____
_____
_____

9. What does the Bible teach us to do when demons attack us?

10. Has God given us authority over demons? Who has this authority?

11. Does Satan have powers? What verses in the Bible indicate the power Satan has?

12. One of my former pastors said he used to warn his family when he went to war with hell. He said there were instances in his house where when he was in the midst of ousting demons in his community and his refrigerator at home would shake violently. What do we need to do to prepare for battle when we know we are entering a battle with the enemy?

13. What does it mean to see with spiritual eyes?

Chapter 4

Demons Smell Death

Demons hate us and want to lead us down a path that leads to hell.

1. Why does Satan tempt us?

2. How do we fight off temptation? How did Jesus?

3. What do you consider idol worship?

4. Do you have things that you put above God?

_____
_____
_____
_____
_____
_____
_____
_____
_____

5. Is it a sin to be angry? When did Jesus become angry?

_____
_____
_____
_____
_____
_____
_____
_____
_____

6. Why should we watch our tongue especially when we are angry?

7. There are those who say that outside variables (such as drugs and alcohol) causes people to do things they would not normally do. Do you think that these outside variables show the "true nature" of a person that they can no longer hide behind when their guard is down? Why or why not? How does Luke 6:45 relate to this question?

8. What are some of the signs of a demon possessed person? Could some of these symptoms also be related to mental illness? How can you test to see if a person is demon possessed?

9. What causes anger in your life that causes you to sin? Is there things you need to give up? (idols). Are there people who draw you into gossip that stirs your anger? When you listen to certain radio shows do you become angry with government or organizations? Write out a step by step plan of how to conquer this area in your life. (Example, I will not engage in gossip. If someone starts talking bad about someone I will tell them that I will not talk about someone behind their back and if they keep it up I will walk away.)

_____
_____
_____
_____
_____
_____
_____
_____
_____
_____
_____
_____
_____
_____

Chapter 5

Heaven or Hell

This chapter addresses what the Bible tells us about heaven and hell.

1. What comes to mind when someone mentions the word heaven? How do you picture heaven?

_____
_____
_____
_____
_____
_____
_____
_____
_____
_____
_____
_____
_____

2. **How do you comprehend eternity as a time element?**

_____
_____
_____
_____
_____
_____
_____
_____
_____
_____
_____
_____
_____
_____
_____
_____
_____

3. **Has God ever given you a vision of heaven? If not have you read books or listen to other testimonies about heaven? If yes what in these stories stood out in your mind?**

_____
_____
_____

4. Besides seeing God and Jesus, what do you look forward to the most?

5. According to Galatians 5:19-21 who will not inherit the kingdom of God?

6. How does the Bible describe hell?

7. When you see your family, your neighbors, the clerk at the grocery store do you ever really get concerned about these people going to hell?

8. Who was hell created for?

9. Do you believe a loving God would truly let people go to hell? Why or Why not?

10. Who determines what sin is?

11. Can God be in the presence of sin? Why or why not?

12. Do you truly know where you are going to go when you die? Do you know if those around are going to heaven or not? How can you be assured a place in heaven?

Chapter 6

Angels and Demons

This chapter explains what the Bible tells us about angels and demons.

1. Do you believe in angels and demons? Why or why not?

   _____
   _____
   _____
   _____
   _____
   _____
   _____
   _____
   _____
   _____

2. What Bible stories do you think about the most when thinking about angels?

   _____
   _____

3. What are the specific jobs of angels?

4. Why do you think God uses angels?

5. What is a demon?

6. What does it mean when it says demons can appear as angels of light?

7. What message do demons spread?

8. Have you ever encountered evil? What did you do?

9. Has the "Hollywood" version of demons skewed our perception of demons?

10. How can reading or watching ghost stories, playing with Ouija boards, tarot cards, etc. invite demons into our lives?

11. Just as the man was distracted by that $100 bill on the highway, we can become distracted by everyday occurrences that get our eyes off God and onto our problems or idols. What things, whether good or bad, can lead to distractions and how can we learn to overcome them?

Chapter 7

Demons Fight for Their Prize

This chapter discusses Satan and the power and influence he can have over us IF we allow it.

1. The war between LuAnn's flesh and her spirit was clearly evident in the letter written in the beginning of the chapter? What are some ways that we can overcome our fleshly desires during troubled times?

_____
_____
_____
_____
_____
_____
_____
_____

2. LuAnn states several times that she called out to God for help, but why do you think she was not feeling the comfort or presence of God?

3. LuAnn states in her letter she "tried to be good" but always failed. Why can't we be "good" on our own?

4. How does this chapter clearly show why we should not give the devil a foothold?

5. Where in your life have you given the devil a foothold? How can you get it back?

6. Write a letter to yourself in the past and warn yourself just before you gave into a temptation that caused problems in your life. Be sure to include all the bad things that could have been avoided if you had not sinned. If you have never done anything serious to effect your life, take a present or past temptation and warn yourself of the effects if you gave into that sin. (This is also a good exercise anytime you face temptation).

Chapter 8

The Journey Home

Even when we are lost and far from God he never stops loving us.

Read Luke 15:11-32 The story of the lost son.

1. How does this story tie into LuAnn's story in this chapter?

   _____
   _____
   _____
   _____
   _____
   _____
   _____
   _____

2. **How does this story truly show God's love for us?**

3. **Is there any wrong we could commit that Jesus could not forgive?**

4. **Do you think you can change a person? Why or why not?**

5. **What is a co-dependent? Can you think of an area that you may be a co-dependent to another person?**

6. Sometimes it feels like everyone has turned their back on us but are we ever truly all alone? Why?

7. How and why does God use our circumstances to get our attention?

8. Write about a specific time God helped you when you seemed to hit rock bottom?

Chapter 9

The Acceptance of Christ

This chapter contains the message of Salvation, what that means and doesn't mean to a believer, and the impact it has when facing evil forces.

1. According to John 3:16 God loved the world so much he gave us His one and only Son. What does that mean to you?

   _____
   _____
   _____
   _____
   _____
   _____
   _____
   _____
   _____

2. What does it mean to be saved?

3. How do you know that you are saved?

4. Once you are saved does that mean that Satan will no longer bother you?

5. Once you are saved does that mean you are going to live a problem free life?

6. Christianity should be relation based not rule based. What does that mean?

7. In what capacity does the law fit into our relation based Christianity?

8. What exactly is sin?

9. Who chooses what is right and wrong?

10. Can God be in the presence of sin? Why or why not?

11. Does evil feed off evil? Give an example. How should we repay evil?

12. The two greatest commandments are to love the Lord your God with all your heart and mind and soul and to love your neighbor as yourself. How then do we see the law if we us the Bible as our standard by which to live?

Chapter 10

The Armor of God

This chapter shows how God equips the believer against the attacks of Satan.

1. In Ephesians 6:10-18 warns us to put on the full armor of God? Why?

2. Whom do we struggle against?

3. Does Satan have more power than humans? Which angel would not challenge Satan but rebuked him in the name of Jesus?

4. What does the belt of truth stand for and why do we need it when fighting against the spiritual forces of evil?

5. What does the breastplate of righteousness stand for and why do we need it when fighting against the spiritual forces of evil?

6. Why do we need our feet fitted with readiness that comes from the gospel of peace?

7. What does the shield of faith stand for and why do we need it when fighting against the spiritual forces of evil?

_____
_____
_____
_____
_____
_____
_____
_____
_____

8. What does the helmet of salvation stand for and why do we need it when fighting against the spiritual forces of evil?

_____
_____
_____
_____

9. What does the sword of the spirit stand for and why do we need it when fighting against the spiritual forces of evil?

10. After we have put on our armor there is one more thing God instructs us to do. What is it and why?

11. Why is it important to be fully equipped when fighting against the spiritual forces of evil?

Chapter 11

The Final Battle

This chapter explains why we should always seek the things of God and not dwell on evil or worldly concepts.

1. According to Matthew 12:43-45 what happens if a person who accepts Christ does not fill his or her thoughts, mind and spirit with the things of the Lord.

2. How can we use Philippians 4:8 in accordance with 12:43-45.

_____
_____
_____
_____
_____
_____
_____
_____
_____
_____

3. According to 1 Samuel 16:14 King Saul was tormented by an evil spirit, yet when David played his harp (verse 23) the evil spirit would leaved him. Why do you think the music helped King Saul?

_____
_____
_____
_____

4. Read 1 Corinthians 5:5 it talks about a man who is to be delivered over to Satan. Why did God allow this man to be handed over to Satan?

5. How can God's glory be revealed in the times he does allow Satan to torment us? Reflect on other stories in the Bible where God allowed Satan to torment people such as Job and Ananias and Sapphira.

6. How do we let the enemy into our homes daily and how can we protect ourselves from such attacks?

7. Write a plan next time evil tries to enter your house, or your thoughts (when a fight breaks out between children, your spouse comes home in a bad mood, etc.) How can you loving implement this plan? Practice so you do not let your emotions override your plan.

_____
_____
_____
_____
_____
_____
_____
_____
_____
_____
_____
_____
_____
_____
_____
_____

Chapter 12

It Is Finished

"Death is swallowed up in victory.

O death, where is thy sting?

O grave, where is thy victory?"

1 Corinthians 15:54-55 (KJV)

1. In today's society death seems to hide behind hospital doors. Have you ever been with a loved one when they died? Looking back how did you cope?

_____
_____
_____
_____
_____
_____
_____

2. When is death swallowed up in victory and when is it a defeat?

_____
_____
_____
_____
_____
_____
_____
_____
_____
_____

3. Why does God allow Satan to cause problems for Christians? (Romans 5:3-5).

_____
_____
_____
_____
_____

4. Explain why our faith becomes works.

5. Do you have a hard time letting others use the Word of God to rebuke (scold) or reprove (admonish) you? Harsh words, yet Nathan rebuked David when he sinned. Do you have a hard time when Jesus instructs you to rebuke or reprove others? (2 Timothy 4:1-5, 2 Timothy 3:16). How is this used as a tool of Satan?

_____

_____

_____

_____

_____

_____

_____

_____

_____

_____

6. What did Jesus mean when He said "It is finished."?

_____

_____

_____

7. We are not assured tomorrow but only today. Write down some stories you have experienced or seen on the news about people dying doing their normal everyday activities.

Conclusion

We hope that completing this Bible study helped you to find answers about how to fight against the enemy as well as strengthen your relationship with Christ and fellow believers. We hope that you take these questions and exercises to heart so when you are faced with evil you will know how to fight against these dark forces with the power and authority God has equipped all the saints. Put on your armor and pray before every battle. It is very important to make sure you are pure and holy before God, for it is only through Him and His power and authority that we can truly conquer evil.

For more information visit our website at:

www.Bibledrivenministries.org

Our blog:

http://bibledrivenministries.wordpress.com

Or follow us on: Twitter or Facebook

Bible Driven Ministries
P.O. Box 1215
Bend, OR 97702

Email: Bibledrivenministries@yahoo.com

www.ingramcontent.com/pod-product-compliance
Lightning Source LLC
Chambersburg PA
CBHW071617040426
42452CB00009B/1373